PRINTHOUSE BOOKS PRESENTS

Now Look Who's Cooking
A Culinary Lifestyle Guide

Darrell 'DAS' Smith

VIP INK Publishing Group, Inc.
Atlanta, GA.

Editor: Natosha Kennedy

ISBN: 978-5323-4887-7

Library of Congress Cataloging-in-Publication Data
LCCN #20179488739

1. Culinary 2. Cook Book
2. Food 4.Darrell 'DAS' Smith 5.Chef

Printed in the United States of America

"Chef DAS"

Copyright © 2017 by Darrell A. Smith II

All rights reserved. This publication is protected by copyright, and permission should be obtained from the publisher prior to any prohibited reproduction, or transmission in any form or by any means, electronic, mechanical, photocopying, recording or likewise without prior permission of the author.

Cover Art by Jamaal "Future" Mashack

Printed and Bound in the United States of America.

**Strength:
The state, property, or quality of being strong.**

To my nephew Brandon: Your strength empowers me every day. I dedicate this book to you.

"Chef DAS"

To My Mother…You are my number one fan and my greatest support system. The reason I am who I am today. The love you have for our family is incomparable. I know raising a young man could not be easy for you, yet you never let me see your struggle. The sacrifices you made to raise your children I now understand and I will never forget them. Our mother son relationship is like no other. I am the mama's boy everyone called me growing up and boy am I proud of it! I thank you, yet a million 'thank yous' wouldn't be enough. I love you with every fiber in my body and hope I served you proud. Please know that your sacrifices were for a bigger purpose and it helped mold my life to the man I am today.

To My Father…My stride, personality, and my want to make people feel good, I owe to you. Growing up I watched you sell water to a well with such ease and confidence. The way people felt around you is something that I always admired and often emulate. I know all things are possible because you instilled that in me. While I was growing up, people would take one look at me and know you were my father. Life shifted you in different directions for various reasons but you always stayed true. I am extremely proud to say that I am your son and I promise to strive to be the best man I can be and do your name proud.

To My Siblings Alonda, Carlos, Sesilee, Cedric, and Abrile…I could not ask for a better set of sisters and brothers. Our parents did a wonderful job of making sure we were there for each other through thick and thin. Each of you have taught, loved, inspired, motivated, and saved me in some way. I am proud of all of you and I love you dearly. Know that I am always here for you as you are for me.

To Chef Kevin Mitchell…Thank you for giving me my first cooking job and believing in me. You saw things in me that I was yet to see for myself. You taught me what a professional chef looked like and to this day when I am in the kitchen I always think what Chef Kevin would do. You are and will always be a true friend and elite master of your craft.

Special Thanks to Martha Bloomfield, Jamaal "Future" Mashack, Jasmine Arizmendi, President Michael Sorrell, Chef William Bloxsom-Carter, Malik Yoba, and lastly but not least Jimmy Benavides.

Finally and most importantly to my wife Jasmine… Thank you for always being my rock in this thing called life your support, unconditional love, and very tolerable patience with me molds me daily as a man and I couldn't imagine a better life partner. Your love and encouragement in the end is what made this book possible.

To my daughter Kennedy… On June 30, 2016 at 5:51pm our lives changed forever you are my biggest motivation in life and every single day that I wake up I strive to make you proud.

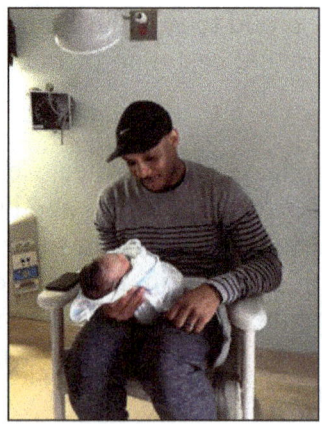

"Chef DAS"

In Memory of

Jasper L. Smith
Clarence O. Davis
Evelyn D. Bowman- Davis

About Chef DAS

Chef Darrell 'DAS' Smith – celebrity chef, author, and teacher – was born and raised in Ypsilanti, Michigan where he learned most of his cooking skills from his mother.
His love for food and the culinary arts began to further develop at the age of 19 while training at Atlanta Technical College, where he focused on American cuisine. It wouldn't be long before Chef DAS would take his talents to the west coast where his unique culinary flair would be at home amongst the palm trees, beaches, and celebrities of Los Angeles, CA.
Chef DAS's commitment to sharing his love for food through education, his invigorating energy, and his undeniable ability to attract an audience of young adults led him to create and helm a one-of-a-kind culinary arts program at Beverly Hills High School.
Among some of Chef DAS's crowning achievements include being hand-selected to cook for the First Lady of the United States, Michelle Obama, at her annual luncheon. Chef DAS has starred in several episodes on the Food Network's hit shows "Next Food Network Star" and "The Great Food Truck Race". He is one of only a handful of chefs to serve as a recurring expert on the Oprah Winfrey Network's hit series, "Home Made Simple." Chef DAS recently had the privilege of calling multi-millionaire entertainer and entrepreneur Sean "Diddy" Combs boss for two years as his full-time personal chef.
 Because of this passion he is dedicating much of his time to creating additional educational programming through books, seminars, television and more.

"Chef DAS"

CONTENTS

Introduction 10
Chapter I Guide to the Grocery Store 12
Chapter II Setting up Your First Kitchen 26
Chapter III Basic Cooking Methods and Language 30
Chapter IV Food Safety 37
Chapter V Knives and Cuts 41
Chapter VI Working with Meat 49
Chapter VII Lifestyle and Nutrition 56
Chapter VIII An Apple a Day Will Keep the Doctor Away 63
Chapter IX Eating Out 69
Chapter X How Long Does It Live 73
Chapter XI Breakfast 80
Chapter XII Lunch 90
Chapter XIII Dinner 100
Afterword 110

Introduction

Leaving the nest behind is a big transition, one that no doubt has you excited and pre-occupied by all kinds of important new important endeavors. Chances are that none of them involve what you are going to eat or how you are going to feed yourself, but these are important issues to consider.

Why? Aside from the obvious fact that you are going to have to eat multiple times every day, food will impact your life in more ways than you realize. With that in mind, this book is more than a basic cookbook. It's a culinary lifestyle guide designed for young adults leaving the safe-haven of their mom's kitchen for the very first time. If you are already out on your own, this book is for you too!

Nowadays, most people skip the food-independence phase of establishing themselves. What I mean by that is many young people eat out most of the time and then make do with pre-packaged, relatively instant unhealthy meals the rest of time. They know only a handful of recipes and probably use pre-made foods as a base for their cooking but left to their own devices, they could not make a wholesome, homemade meal even if you put all the ingredients right in front of them. Because of this, restaurants and pre-packaged foods are not just a convenience anymore. They've become a whole way of life. Young people are dependent on them.

Restaurants are amazing and ready-made foods can be lifesavers, but people should not have to depend on them because they do not know any other way. After all, it is because of our reliance on these low quality, processed foods and too-rich, too-massive, restaurant portions that we've become obese and disease ridden as a general population. This book will teach you not only the basic necessities of cooking, but also sanitation, safety and methods of preparation. It will also provide a glimpse into practical nutrition and how to make the most of your money. The delicious recipes I have included are ones you can cook in any setting, whether you have a full kitchen or are stuck in a dorm room making due with a mini-fridge, a hot plate and toaster oven.

All the recipes in this book meet the following criteria:

- They include little prep and cook time.
- They are inexpensive and budget conscious.
- They are simple and straightforward.
- They are things you're actually interested in eating.
- They are absolutely, mouth-wateringly delicious!

CHAPTER I
Guide to the Grocery Store

"Chef DAS"

The funny thing is that when I was younger I never really enjoyed going to the grocery store. Following my mother around knowing her intent was not to buy me anything was not my idea of a good time. Now that I'm an adult and understand the need and the quality of each ingredient needed to prepare a meal I cannot wait to go to shopping. Believe me when I tell you that after you read this book you will not be able to wait either.

Life is about choices and this is exactly how I see grocery shopping. Think of the store as a huge palace with infinite options. As with everything though, you must have a plan. It's important that you create a menu/meal plan before you go shopping to ensure that you stock your shelves with food that makes sense. This book will show you the How's and Why's of proper food selection.

When shopping for food you must consider two very important factors: how much time do you have to prepare and how much energy do you want to put into the meal? Other factors to consider are the nutrition of the food but also how much money you want to spend on food. Most of the time some of these factors become trade-offs.

While grocery shopping on a budget, save your grocery receipts to keep an accurate track of the food you are purchasing. Proteins tend to be the most costly of the food groups but can vary in price and selection. Fruits and vegetables are next when it comes to cost. Fresh fruits and vegetables in comparison to frozen and canned ones tend to be the most economical when in season. However, during the off-season, frozen and canned ones tend to be cheaper.

When buying fresh fruit and vegetables, follow these helpful lists to ensure you are making the best selections. The following information contains the peak seasons of each fruit and vegetable. However, that does not mean you cannot find them at other times of the calendar year.

Selecting Fresh Fruit

Apples: Peak Season September-May
Search for: Firm, crisp, well-colored apples. Flavor varies in apples, and depends on the stage of maturity at the time that the fruit is picked. Apples must be mature when picked to have a good flavor, texture, and storing ability. Immature apples lack color and are usually poor in flavor.
Stay away from: Overripe apples, and apples affected by freeze which is normally indicated by bruises.

Apricots: Peak Season June-July
Search for: Apricots that are plump and juicy looking, with a golden-orange color.
Stay away from: Dull-looking, soft or mushy fruit, and very firm, or greenish yellow fruit.

Avocados: Peak Season All Year
Search for: If you plan on using immediately select soft avocados that seem a little mushy if you squeeze a bit.

For use in a few days, buy more firm fruits. Leave out at room temperature to ripen.
Stay away from: Avocados that have dark spots, or cracked or broken surfaces. These are signs of decay.

Bananas: Peak Season All Year
Search for: Bananas which are firm, bright in appearance, and free from bruises or other injury. The best way to determine the ripeness of a banana is the skin color. For the best flavor, the skin color should be bright yellow with small speckles. Bananas with green tips are not yet ripe and should be left out at room temperature.
Stay away from: Bruised fruit, discolored skins; dull or over aged looking.

Blackberries/Blueberries: Peak Season June-August
Search for: Blackberries/Blueberries that are plump, firm, uniform in size, dry, and free from stems or leaves.
Stay away from: Soft, mushy, or leaking berries.

Cherries: Peak Season May-June
Search for: Cherries that have a very dark color is the main indication that the cherries are sweet and have good flavor. Good cherries have bright, glossy, plump-looking surfaces and fresh-looking stems.
Stay away from: Shriveling, dried stems, and a generally dull appearance. Soft, leaking flesh, brown discoloration, and mold growth are also indications of decay.

Coconuts: Peak Season September-March
Search for: Coconuts that have a good weight for the size, make sure the milk inside is still liquid, if not liquid coconut is spoiled.
Stay away from: Coconuts that look wet.

Cranberries: Peak Season September-January
Search for: Plump, firm berries with dark red color, which generally provides the best flavor.
Stay away from: Brown, dark, and discolored berries and soft, spongy, or leaky berries.

Figs: Peak Season July-September
Search for: Figs that have a rich, deep color and are plump and tender, but not mushy. Be sure to use soon after purchase as they spoil quickly.
Stay away from: Figs that smell sour or do not have stems.

Grapefruit: Peak Season All Year
Search for: Firm fruits, heavy for their size. Grapefruit that has thin skinned has the most juice. If a grapefruit is pointed at the stem end, it is likely to be thick-skinned.
Stay away from: Soft, water-soaked areas, and lack of bright color.

Grapes: Peak Season June-December
Search for: Well-colored, plump grapes firmly attached to the stem. Green grapes tend to be tarter, while red grapes tend to be a bit sweeter. Bunches are more likely to hold together if the stems are green.
Stay away from: Soft or wrinkled grapes, or bunches of grapes with stems that are brown.

Kiwi: Peak Season June-August
Search for: Plump, unwrinkled fruit. Kiwi fruit is fully ripe when it's firm to touch but not soft. If kiwi is too hard when purchased it can ripen at home in a few days by leaving it out at room temperature.
Stay away from: Fruit that shows signs of wrinkling, mold, or mush.

Lemons: Peak Season All Year
Search for: Lemons with a bright yellow color, smooth skin with a slight gloss, and those that are firm and heavy.
Stay away from: Lemons with a darker yellow or dull color, or with hardened or wrinkled skin.

Limes: Peak Season May-October (Available All Year)
Search for: Limes with glossy skin and heavy weight for the size.
Stay away from: Limes with dull, dry skin and those with soft spots, mold, and skin punctures.

Mangoes: Peak Season April-August
Search for: Mangoes that are not too soft. Mangoes can vary in size ranging from a plum to a grapefruit. Colors are often red and yellow with some spots of black. Smell the stem for a fruity aroma.
Stay away from: Mangoes that smell sour or like alcohol. The alcohol smell is a sure sign that the mango is overripe.

Melons:
Cantaloupes: Peak Season May-September
Search for: Cantaloupes where the stem is gone, leaving smooth symmetrical base. The veining should be

thick and coarse. A ripe cantaloupe will have a yellowish color to the rind, and have a pleasant cantaloupe aroma.
Stay away from: Cantaloupes that have a soft rind. Mold growth on the cantaloupe.

Honeydews: Peak Season February-October
Search for: Honeydews that have a soft texture, a pleasant fruit aroma, and yellowish-white rind color indicate ripeness.
Stay away from: Greenish-white color. Melons that are too hard are signs of maturity.

Watermelons: Peak Season May-September
Search for: Firm, juicy flesh with bright red color and seeds that are dark brown or black. Seedless watermelons often contain small white seeds. Also look for the ground spot, which is the spot on the bottom that should be a creamy yellow color. If it's white or slightly green the watermelon was probably picked too soon and is not completely ripe. The watermelon should be dull and symmetrical in shape and smooth.
Stay away from: Melons with pale-colored flesh, white streaks, and a greenish-white ground spot.

Nectarines: Peak Season June-September
Search for: Rich color and plumpness. Most varieties have an orange-yellow color between the red areas.
Stay away from: Hard, dull fruits or slightly wrinkled skin.

Oranges: Peak Season All Year

Search for: Firm and heavy oranges with fresh, bright looking skin that is reasonably smooth.
Stay away from: Oranges that have very rough skin texture. Dull, dry skin and spongy texture also indicates flesh without flavor.

Peaches: Peak Season May-November
Search for: Peaches that are fairly firm. The skin color should be between yellow and red.
Stay away from: Very firm or hard peaches which are probably immature and won't ripen properly. Also avoid very soft fruits that are overripe.

Pears: Peak Season August-November
Search for: Pears that are hard but have already begun to soften.
Stay away from: Wilted or wrinkled pears with dull-appearing skin. Also avoid spots on the sides or blossom ends of the pear.

Pineapples: Peak Season March-June (Available All Year)
Search for: Bright color, and a very slight separation of the eyes. Pineapples are usually dark green, firm, and heavy for their size. When fully colored, pineapples are golden yellow, orange-yellow, or reddish brown, depending on the variety. Signs of ripeness are when leaves are easily removed.
Stay away from: Pineapples with sunken or slightly pointed pips, or bruised fruit, discolored or soft spots, and eyes that are dark and watery.

Plums: Peak Season June-September
Search for: Plums with a good color and firmness.

Stay away from: Fruits with skin breaks, hard, poorly colored, and sometimes wrinkled.

Strawberries: Peak Season March-July
Search for: Berries with a bright red color, firm flesh, and the stem cap still attached. The berries should be dry and clean, and usually small to medium small strawberries have better eating quality than large ones.
Stay away from: Berries with large leaking areas, or those with mold, which can spread rapidly from one berry to another.

Tangerines: Peak Season November-March Search for: Deep bright orange color is your best sign of fresh, good-flavored tangerines. Tangerine skins are normally pretty loose so they frequently will not feel firm to the touch.
Stay away from: Very pale yellow and puffy skin.

Selecting Fresh Vegetables

Artichokes: Peak Season March-May
Search for: Globes that are deep green with a tight leaf formation and that are heavy for their size. A good way to detect freshness is to press leaves together, which should produce a squeaking sound.
Stay away from: Artichokes that appear dry or moldy.

Asparagus: Peak Season March-June
Search for: Bundles that are bright green with closed, compact firm tips. Try to buy bundles that are equally thick to ensure they will cook evenly.
Stay away from: Spread out open tips and angular or ridged spears. Also avoid moldy or decayed tips.

Beets: Peak Season June-October
Search for: Firm, round, smooth surfaced and rich in color. Main judge of freshness comes from the tops of the beets.
Stay away from: Wilted or decayed tops, also long roots with scaly areas on surface they tend to be tough.

Belgian Endive: Peak Season October-May
Search for: Firm leaves without bruises. Green-white color.
Stay away from: Brown or wet leaves.

Broccoli: Peak Season October-May
Search for: Select stalks that are dark green firm and tight.
Stay away from: Broccoli that has an odor or a yellowish green color to the heads this indicates that it's old.

Brussels sprouts: Peak Season October-December
Search for: Fresh, bright green color, miniature and compact heads.
Stay away from: Loose fitting outer leaves and blemishes.

Cabbage: Peak Season All Year
Search for: Heads that are firm and compact. Leaves should be crispy and free of damage. The darker the leaves, the more flavor the cabbage will have.
Stay away from: Precut or shredded cabbage. Once cabbage is cut, it begins to lose the vitamin C content.

Carrots: Peak Season All Year
Search for: Firm; plump, bright colored, smooth and free of cracks. Best to buy in bunches with leafy green tops still attached.
Stay away from: Rough, cracked, wilted roots or tops.

Cauliflower: Peak Season September-November
Search for: Clean creamy white florets that have bright green leaves surrounding. Sizes can vary.
Stay away from: Spotted, discolored or bruised florets.

Celery: Peak Season All Year
Search for: Celery that is light green in color, firm, compact, and well-shaped. Also, look for stalks that are glossy and leaflets are fresh.
Stay away from: Celery that has bruises, blemishes or wilted stems.

Corn: Peak Season May-September
Search for: Bright green moist husks, Plump milky shiny kernels. You should be able to feel individual kernels. The silk should be stiff.
Stay away from: Cobs with small or large dented kernels.

Cucumbers: Peak Season May-August
Search for: Bright, shiny green; firm; and well-shaped.
Stay away from: Wet, moldy or mushy appearance.

Eggplant: Peak Season August-September
Search for: Firm smooth skinned dark purple eggplant that is heavy for its size. Smaller eggplants usually have the best flavor.
Stay away from: Soft or brown spots.

Garlic: Peak Season All Year
Search for: Big, plump and firm.
Stay away from: Spongy texture, soft or wrinkled skin.

Green Beans: Peak Season May-October
Search for: Slender beans that are crisp and bright green.
Stay away from: Brown, broken beans that are exposed.

Kale: Peak Season August-January
Search for: Fresh kale will have a deep green hue and moist, hardy stems.
Stay away from: Leaves that are wilted, browned, or have small holes in them.

Lettuce: Peak Season All Year
Search for: Fresh crisp leaves, medium weight for size.
Stay away from: Bruised or wilted leaves.

Mushrooms: Peak Season November-April
Search for: Dry, clean, firm caps and stems.
Stay away from: Mushrooms that are moldy or soft. Also avoid open and discolored caps.

Okra: Peak Season May-September
Search for: Tender bright green pods that are ¾ inches long and should be firm and moist.
Stay away from: Spotted, moldy limp or dry pods.

Onions: Peak Season All Year
Search for: Onions that are heavy for their size with dry, papery skins.
Stay away from: Onions that have a smell, soft or sprouting.

Peas: Peak Season April-July
Search for: Pods that are firm and smooth, bright green in color and slightly swollen.
Stay away from: Pods that color is distorted with speckles of grey.

Peppers: Peak Season All Year
Search for: Great shape; firm exterior, smooth glossy skin with no bruises.
Stay away from: Wet moldy skin, and cracked surfaces.

Potatoes: Peak Season All Year
Search for: Fairly smooth, well-shaped, firm and free of blemishes.
Stay away from: Bruised, sprouting, wrinkled skin or green surface.

Radishes: Peak Season May-July
Search for: Medium sized bright red color. Plump, round and firm.
Stay away from: Wilted tops, pink-white color.

Spinach: Peak Season March-May
Search for: Large crisp bright green leaves free of blemishes.
Stay away from: Leaves with coarse stems, also those that are limp, damaged or spotted.

Squash (summer): Peak Season June-August
Search for: Squash that are tender and well-shaped, firm, bright color, smooth with glossy skin.
Stay away from: Dull appearance, also hard or tough surface.

Squash (winter): Peak Season: September-November
Search for: Hard rind, also heavy for its size.

Stay away from: Squash with cuts, punctures or moldy spots.

Sweet Potato: Peak Season: September- December
Search for: Firm potatoes with smooth skin, free from any signs of decay.
Stay away from: Any wormholes, cuts, or punctures.

Tomatoes: Peak Season: May- August (Available All Year)
Search for: Well formed; plump, bright in color and smooth skin.
Stay away from: Wormholes and tomatoes that are soft in spots.

Chapter II
Setting Up Your First Kitchen

"Chef DAS"

Setting up for your first kitchen can be very exciting. If possible, buy cookware that you know will last. Nowadays, you can find inexpensive cookware that will work as well as the expensive ones. Always remember, it is the quality and not the quantity that counts. In this chapter you will learn not only the proper utensils and cookware you will need to set up your kitchen but also the proper way to use them.

Cutting Board: are used to protect countertops.

Colander: is used to drain water from foods.

Dry measuring cups: are used to measure dry, moist, or solid ingredients.

Grater: is used to shred food into smaller pieces.

Kitchen fork: is used to lift and turn large cuts of meat.

Knives: are used to cut food in different sizes. A decent set of knives is a must have. Most of the time you can purchase your knife and cutting board in the same section.

Ladles: are used to serve soups or stews.

Liquid measuring cups: are used to measure liquid ingredients.

Measuring spoons: are used to measure small amounts of ingredients.

Mixing Bowls: are used for mixing, also serving and are usually made of stainless steel, glass, or ceramic.

Non-stick pans, 6 inch and 8 inch: are used for all types of cooking and are more helpful because of the coating it prevents food from sticking.

Non-Stick Sauce pan: A deep pan with a handle; used for stewing or boiling, usually comes with a lid. The lid is used when you want to keep the moisture of the food inside. (steam)

Peeler: A peeler cuts a thin layer from vegetables and fruits more efficiently than a paring knife does. Peelers have a swiveling blade that moves over pieces of food. With a very sharp blade, it peels when used in an upward and downward motion.

Pizza Cutter: is used to cut pizzas and pies.

Rubber Spatula: is also sometimes called a scraper because it's used to scrape the inside of bowls and pans ensuring no food are ever wasted.

Sauté pan: is a shallow, multipurpose pan that comes in two different shapes. Sometimes it's referred to as a skillet.

Spoons: Spoons are used for mixing, stirring, scooping, and serving foods. They may be wooden or stainless steel and may also be solid or slotted.

Tongs: Tongs are used to pick up very hot items, but also used while serving food to other people as a sanitary tool.

Whisk: A whisk is a hand tool with thin wires in a round shape. It's used to add air to mixtures. Whisks and whips are very similar and primarily do the same thing. The only difference is that whips have thicker wires and provide less air while blending.

Lastly get yourself some small appliances that pack big punches like a good toaster and blender. Believe me there will be a time when your creativity will have to take over and the meals you can make with these small appliances will amaze you and others. To finish your kitchen off you'll need a set of cutlery and plates. Once you have these items familiarize yourself with your kitchen. Take a step back and look around. Think about all the wonderful meals you will be creating in this space.

**Chapter III
Basic Cooking Methods and
Language**

In this chapter you will learn basic cooking methodology and terminology. You will often come across words that will look and sound foreign. Do not get discouraged. I have been there and that is why I created your terminology bible. After reading this section you will have all you need to know to begin your culinary journey.

Bake: To cook in oven with dry heat.

Barbeque: To cook on a rack or spit over hot coals or some other source of direct heat.

Baste: To spoon pan juices, melted fat or another liquid over the surface of food during cooking to keep the food moist and add flavor.

Beat: To mix ingredients together with a circular up and down motion using a spoon, whisk, or rotary or electric beater.

Blanch: To scald or parboil (to partially boil) in water or steam.

Blend: To stir ingredients until they are thoroughly combined.

Boil: To cook in liquid at 212°F.

Braise: To cook in a small amount of liquid in a tightly covered pan over low heat.

Broil: To cook uncovered under a direct source of heat.

Caramelize: To heat sugar until a brown color and characteristic flavor develop.

Chop: To cut into small pieces.

Clarify: To make a liquid clear by removing solid particles.

Coat: To thoroughly cover a food with a liquid or dry mixture.

Combine: To mix or blend two or more ingredients.

Cut: To divide into small parts with a sharp utensil.

Deep-fry: To cook in a large amount of hot oil.

Dice: To cut into very small cubes of even size.

Drain: To remove liquid from a food product.

Dredge: To coat a food by sprinkling it with or dipping it in a dry ingredient such as flour or bread crumbs.

Flour: To sprinkle or coat with flour.

Garnish: To decorate foods by adding other attractive and complementary food to the serving dish.

Glaze: To apply a liquid that forms a glossy coating.

Grate: To reduce a food into small bits by rubbing it on the sharp teeth on a utensil.

Grease: To rub fat on the surface of a cooking utensil or on a food itself.

Grill: To broil over hot coals or to fry on a griddle.

Julienne: To cut food into thin, stick-sized strips.

Knead: To work dough by pressing it with the heels of the hands, folding it, turning it, and repeating each motion until the dough is smooth and elastic.

Marinade: To soak meat in a solution containing an acid, such as vinegar or tomato juice, that helps tenderize the connective tissue.

Mash: To break food by pressing it with the back of a spoon or masher.

Mince: To cut or chop into very fine pieces.

Mix: To combine two or more ingredients into one mass.

Pan broil: To cook without fat in an uncovered skillet.

Panfry: To cook in a skillet with a small amount of fat.

Parboil: To boil in liquid until partially cooked.

Peel: To remove the outer layer.

Poach: To cook over or in a simmering liquid.

Preheat: To heat an appliance to a desired temperature before using.

Reduce: To decrease the quantity of a liquid and intensify the flavor by boiling.

Roast: To cook uncovered in the oven with dry heat.

Sear: To brown the surface of a food very quickly with high heat.

Season: To add herbs, spices, or other ingredients to a food to increase the flavor of the food.

Sift: To put through a sieve to reduce to finer particles.

Simmer: To cook in a liquid that is barely at the boiling point.

Slice: To cut thin, flat pieces.

Steam: To cook with vapor produced by a boiling liquid.

Stew: To cook one food or several foods together in a seasoned liquid for a long period.

Stir-fry: To cook foods quickly in a small amount of fat over high heat while stirring constantly.

Thicken: To make a liquid denser by adding an agent like flour, cornstarch, or egg yolks.

Whip: To beat steadily by hand with a whisk or rotary beater.

Abbreviations to know:

Tsp. or t. = teaspoon
Tbsp. or T. = Tablespoon
C. = Cup
pt. = Pint
qt. = Quart
oz. = Ounce
qt. = quart
Gal. =Gallon
Lb. or # = Pound

Metric
ML = Milliliter
L = Liter
G = Gram
Kg = Kilogram
Equivalent Measures:

3 teaspoons = 1 Tablespoon
16 Tablespoons = 1 cup
12 Tablespoons = ¾ cup
8 Tablespoons = ½ cup
4 tablespoons = ¼ cup
2 Tablespoons = 1/8 cup
2 cups = 1 pint
2 pints =1 quart

4 quarts = 1 gallon
1 pound = 16 ounces

MyPlate shows the five food groups that promotes a healthy well balanced diet.

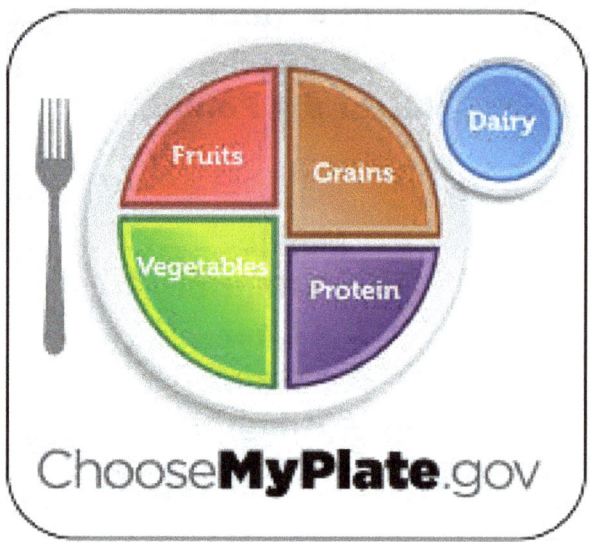

Source: USDA www.choosemyplate.gov

"Chef DAS"

**Chapter IV
Food Safety**

It is important that you create meals that will not make you or others sick. How can you avoid that? The best way to prevent any unsafe food is to create habits when you are cooking like always keeping a clean work area. "Cleanliness is next to Godliness"
(Acts 9:32-10:23).

A food borne illness can contaminate your food from three different types of hazards.

Biological Hazards: include the biological agents found in or on foods that can cause harm to humans. The four basic types of biological hazards are: bacteria, viruses, parasites, and fungi.

Physical Hazards: are foreign objects that usually enter the food at the production stage. Most objects are large enough to see or feel while you are eating such as a piece of plastic, or a piece of glass or metal.

Chemical Hazards: are any chemical substances that are found in food caused by accidents in the home or workplace.

Helping <u>pathogens</u> (germs) grow rapidly when conditions are right in foods. Some foods offer a friendly environment for growth. These foods are referred to as potentially hazardous foods.

Leaving food in the food danger zone which means pathogens grow in temperatures from 41°F to 135°F. (Think about the days when you would go to your grandmother's house and she would leave her Sunday's dinner out. Well, those days are over).

Sources of contamination: can come in two ways, by direct contamination or by cross-contamination.

Direct contamination: occurs when one type of raw food touches or drips onto a cooked food item. This can happen by incorrect use of utensils or by improperly carrying raw food over cooked food.

Cross contamination: is the transfer of harmful bacteria to any food in the   prepping, or cooking, or serving stage. This happens from improperly handled cutting boards, utensils or other foods. The best way to prevent cross contamination is to keep all raw foods separate from cooked food. Ideally, you want to use two separate cutting boards, one for meats and the other for other food products.

Grooming and hygiene are so important. Everyone who works with food needs to make an effort to keep clean, well groomed, and healthy.

This is what my chalkboard looked like in culinary school.

ALWAYS CLEAN AS YOU GO
ALWAYS CLEAN AS YOU GO
ALWAYS CLEAN AS YOU GO
ALWAYS CLEAN AS YOU GO
ALWAYS CLEAN AS YOU GO
ALWAYS CLEAN AS YOU GO
ALWAYS CLEAN AS YOU GO
ALWAYS CLEAN AS YOU GO
ALWAYS CLEAN AS YOU GO
ALWAYS CLEAN AS YOU GO
ALWAYS CLEAN AS YOU GO
ALWAYS CLEAN AS YOU GO
ALWAYS CLEAN AS YOU GO
ALWAYS CLEAN AS YOU GO
ALWAYS CLEAN AS YOU GO
ALWAYS CLEAN AS YOU GO
ALWAYS CLEAN AS YOU GO
ALWAYS CLEAN AS YOU GO
ALWAYS CLEAN AS YOU GO
ALWAYS CLEAN AS YOU GO
ALWAYS CLEAN AS YOU GO
ALWAYS CLEAN AS YOU GO

"Chef DAS"

Chapter V
Knives and Cuts

The knife will be your best friend in your kitchen. It is the number one tool you will use. Make sure you always use a sharp knife. Why? Believe it or not you have a greater chance of harming yourself with a dull knife. Once you become one with your knife, cooking is easy. Be safe!!

Here are the three most common knifes for your home.

Chef's Knife
Also known as a cook's knife, the chef's knife is an all-purpose knife used for slicing, chopping, dicing, mincing, and many other functions. The blade is curved to allow the cook to rock the knife on the cutting board for a more precise cut. Chef's knives are most commonly available between six and twelve inches, though eight inches is the most common size. Most chefs recommend using the largest chef's knife that is comfortable in the cook's hands. Larger knives can cut more and are more versatile, but can be more difficult to handle.

Bread Knife
Bread knives are a type of serrated knife (Serrated knives have blades that look like a saw) Bread knives are usually between six and ten inches. Eight inches is a common length. The serrations on the blade make it ideal for cutting bread (and other things that are hard on the outside and soft on the inside)

Paring Knife
A paring knife is a small knife with a plain edge blade that is ideal for peeling and other small or intricate work (such as deveining a shrimp, removing the seeds from a jalapeno, or cutting small garnishes). It is designed to be an all-purpose knife, similar to a chef's knife, except

smaller. Paring knives are usually between two and a half and four inches, as anything larger than about four or five inches is typically considered a utility knife (although the distinction is somewhat vague).
The four basic grips used with a chef's knife are as follows:

- Grip the handle with all four fingers and hold the thumb gently but firmly against the blade's spine.

- Grip the handle with all four fingers and hold the thumb gently but firmly against the side of the blade.

- Grip the handle with three fingers, rest the index finger flat against the blade on one side, and hold the thumb on the opposite side to give additional stability and control.

- Grip the handle overhand, with the knife held vertically – this grip is used with a boning knife for meat fabrication tasks.

The Control Hand
Your grip on the knife is determined as much by your personal preference and comfort as it is by the cutting tasks, at hand. The same is true for your control hand, the hand responsible for controlling the food you are cutting. Use your controlling hand, the hand not holding the knife, to hold the object that you are cutting. This is done to prevent food from slipping as you cut it. It also makes it easier to control the size of the cut or slice you are making.

Precision Cuts

The aim should always be to cut the food into pieces of uniform shape and size. Evenly cut items look more attractive, but more important, they cook evenly so your dishes have the best possible flavor, color, and texture. Unevenly cut items give an impression of carelessness that can spoil the dish's look.

The flavor, texture, and appearance of the dish suffer if its components are unevenly cut. Most foods require some preliminary trimming, peeling, or squaring off to make subsequent cuts easier to perform.

- Trimming tasks include removing root and stem ends from fruits, herbs, and vegetables.

- Peeling tasks can be done using a rotary peeler if the skin is not too thick. Carrot, potato, and similar skins are easy to remove with a peeler. Remember that these peelers work in both directions.

- Pairing knives can also be used to trim many fruits and vegetables.

- A chef's knife is required for vegetables, fruits and other foods with thick rinds or skins, such as hard-skinned squashes and pineapples.

- Exterior fat, gristle, and sinew (tough tissue) can be removed from meats and poultry with a boning knife.

- Foods that are naturally round can be difficult to control as you cut them.

- A slice can be removed from the bottom or side of a round food to make it sit flat on the cutting board.

Basic Cuts

Chop

Coarse chopping is generally used for mirepoix (celery, onions, carrots) or similar flavoring ingredients that are to be strained out of the dish and discarded. It is also appropriate when cutting vegetables that will be puréed.

- Trim the root and stem ends and peel the vegetables if necessary.

- Slice or cut through the vegetables at nearly regular intervals until the cuts are relatively uniform. This need not be a perfectly neat cut, but all the pieces should be roughly the same size.

Mince

- Mincing is a very fine cut that is suitable for many vegetables and herbs. When mincing herbs, rinse and dry well, and strip the leaves from the stems.

- Put the leaves in a pile on a cutting board.

- Use your control hand to hold them in place and position the knife so that you can slice through the pile; coarsely chop.

- Once the herbs are coarsely chopped, use the fingertips of your guiding hand to hold the tip of the chef's knife in contact with the cutting board.

- Keeping the tip of the blade against the cutting board, lower the knife firmly and rapidly, repeatedly cutting through the herbs. Continue cutting until the desired fineness is attained.

Chiffonade

- The chiffonade cut is done by hand to cut herbs, leafy greens, and other ingredients into very fine shreds. Chiffonade is distinct from shredding, however, in that the cuts are much finer and uniform. This cut is typically for delicate leafy vegetables and herbs such as basil and spinach.

- For greens with large, loose leaves, roll individual leaves into tight cylinders before cutting. Stack several smaller leaves before cutting.

- Use a chef's knife to make very fine, parallel cuts to produce fine shreds.

Julienne & Bàtonnet

- Julienne and bâtonnet are long, rectangular cuts (think of French fries).

- Julienne cuts are 1/8 inch in thickness and 1-2 inches long.

- Bâtonnet cuts are ¼ inch in thickness and 2-2 ½ inches long.

- These dimensions may be modified slightly to suit a specific need. Most importantly, each cut should be nearly identical in dimension to all others for even cooking and the best appearance.

- Trim and square off the vegetable by cutting a slice to make four straight sides. Cut both ends to even the block off. These initial slices make it easier to produce even cuts.
- The trimmings can be used for stocks, soups, purées, or any preparation where shape is not important.

- Slice the vegetable lengthwise, using parallel cuts of the desired thickness.

- Stack the slices, aligning the edges, and make parallel cuts of the same thickness through the stack.

Dice cuts

- Dicing is a cutting technique that produces a cube-shaped product. Different preparations require different sizes of dice - fine brunoise small, medium, and large dice

- The term brunoise is derived from the French verb, brunoir (to brown), and reflects the common practice of sautéing these finely diced vegetables.

- Trim and peel the vegetables as needed.

- Cut the slices to the thickness that you wish the finished dice.

- Stack the slices on top of one another and make even cuts to the appropriate thickness.

- Gather the sticks together using your control hand to hold them in place, and make crosswise parallel cuts through the sticks.

- To produce perfectly even, neat dice, these cuts should be the same thickness as the initial slices

"Chef DAS"

CHAPTER VI
Working with Meat

Meat: The edible flesh of mammals that is eaten as food. Meat is mainly composed of water and protein.

The Benefit of Meat

When looking at the Food Guide Pyramid, it is recommended that you eat two to three daily servings from the meat and beans. The daily consumption of meat should range from 4 to 8 ounces. Meat contains proteins that help build and repair tissue. Meats are also good sources of Iron and Zinc.

At times you will notice certain meat have more fat than others. The amount of fat that meat contributes to the diet relies on the cut and quality. Fat enhances the flavor of meat although not appealing to the eye.

A healthful diet can be attainable by choosing the leaner cuts of meat. For example, choose loin sections of beef and the loin and leg sections of pork rather than a cut from the tenderloin area. Now don't get me wrong, tenderloins are the more flavorful of the bunch but contain the highest fat content. If you choose to use the fattier cut of the meat, use cooking methods like grilling. This allows the fat to drip away.

Choosing Meat

Meat can be very expensive so to ensure you are getting the most for your money you want to make sure you are picking quality product.

The Meat scale goes as follows:

- USDA PRIME
- USDA CHOICE
- USDA SELECT

The appearance of meat is a sure sign of the quality. Marbling (meat that has a marble appearance) indicates tenderness in a cut of meat, although it means more total fat. When grocery shopping on an ordinary day, choose the leaner cuts of meat.

How Much Meat Should I Buy?

The first thing to know is that all meat is sold by the pound. The meat is usually the main event. Therefore, when purchasing the meat you will need to know how many people you will be serving. One thing to look for is the amount of bone in the meat, which can affect your purchase.

Storage Times for Meat

Refrigerated Storage

Meat types	Time
Fresh cuts	3-4 days
Ground meats	1-2 days

Leftover cooked meats   3 days

<u>Freezer Storage</u>
Luncheon meats, hot dogs 2 months
Ham   2 months
Ground meats   3 months
Pork cuts   6 months
Lamb   9 months
Beef   12 months

Methods of Cooking Meat

So let's start cooking! Now, I know cooking meat can be an intimidating, scary task for most but with these six cooking methods you'll be able to hit the kitchen confidently. There are five dry heat methods: roasting; broiling; pan-frying; deep-frying; and grilling which is best for the more tender cuts of the meat.(ex. steak, chicken thighs, and drumsticks). The one moist heat method is braising which is best for the less tender parts (ex. chicken breast, or beef brisket etc.)

Here are a **few** tips to remember for cooking meat safely.

- Always store meats at 32-40 degrees F.
- When handling raw meat always wash your hands before and after.
- When working with raw meat be sure to carefully wash your cutting boards and other utensils before using them on other food products
- Place your meat in the refrigerator to marinate and cover tightly.

"Chef DAS"

- To ensure your meat has reached the proper internal temperature insert a thermometer into the thickest part of the meat.
- Set the oven at 350° degrees or above when cooking meats.

Beef
Rare   120°-125°
Medium-rare   130°-135°
Medium   140°-145°
Medium-well   150°-155°
Well done   160° and above

Lamb
Rare   135°
Medium Rare   140°-150°
Medium   160°
Well done   165° and above

Pork   150°

Poultry
Chicken   165°-175°
Turkey   165°-175°

Roasting (Pre - Heat Your Oven): Roasting also known as baking is recommended for large, tender cuts of meat. When roasting, you always want to sear the meat first which helps develop a golden skin texture. After searing, place the uncovered meat on an oven rack in a pan fat side up. Once the meat has reached the proper internal temperature, take out and allow resting for 10 to 15 minutes. This will make it easier for you to carve.

Broiling & Grilling: When using these methods your selection of meat should be a thicker cut. If meat is too thin it will dry out before it is cooked thoroughly. The only difference between broiling and grilling is that the heat source comes from different directions. When broiling, the direct heat source comes from above. (Usually you will broil in the bottom section of the oven). The closer the meat is to the heat source the quicker it will cook. When grilling, the heat source comes from a direct heat source below. (Usually in an outdoor gas or charcoal barbeque grill). Be sure to season your food first when using these methods. The other distinction between broiling and grilling is that the meat must be turned over when broiling and when grilling, no turning in necessary.

Pan-Fried: The best pan to use for this method is a non-stick pan or skillet. This method is used when cooking a small portion of meat. Pan-fried foods almost always are coated with either flour or breadcrumbs and cooked in just enough oil to cover one half. The selection of meat that work best for this method are lean pieces of chicken, pork or fish.

Deep-Frying: To deep-fry make sure that your pan or pot is big enough for your meat to be completely submerged in oil. When deep- frying you must season the meat before coating with flour or breadcrumbs. It is very important that you preheat the oil to reach 325°-375°F. Make sure not to overheat the oil which will cause the meat to burn before it is cooked internally.

Take the meat out, once it has reached a golden brown color and begins to float. Place it on a paper towel to drain the access oil.

Braising: Braising is cooking in a small amount of liquid over low heat. For best results when braising, season the meat on all sides and sear on high heat until browned. Remove meat from pan and add into pot with liquid such as broth, water, or vegetable juice. The liquid should barely cover the meat. Add ingredients (ex. fresh herbs, celery, carrots etc). Cover the pot tightly and cook slowly on low heat until the meat is tender.

Chapter VII
Lifestyle and Nutrition

The way you treat your body is the way your body will treat you. It is very important to understand the impact of living a healthy lifestyle and the affect that it will have on you.

Family

Today's family spends more time away from the home in order to provide for their families than they did years ago. Not only did this shift affect our health as a society but it also decreased the amount of communication happening in the home. The days of sitting down to a home cooked meal with no distractions are long gone. Between work, school and other extra-curricular activities, who has time for a home cooked meal right? WRONG! I promise you will be able to make a home cooked meal in no time. I say, let's get cooking and let's get talking!

Outside Influences

Be careful of the company you keep. Believe it or not, your friends have an influence on the food you eat. Peer pressure from your friends to eat or try different things happens all the time. Picture this. You are at a pizza shop and all your friends are ordering pizza. Nine times out of ten, you are not going to order the only salad on the menu. If you do, be proud!

Also be mindful of the mass media such as television, radio, magazines, newspapers, and the Internet that also has a major affect on the food you eat. Advertising is a key way that media influences your food choices. Advertisements encourage you to try new food products and also recreate new ads for the old products. The key companies know exactly what they are doing by hiring your favorite celebrities to appear in their commercials while holding their key products. Now, do not get me wrong. It is not a bad thing. Just be careful when watching television and evaluate the message that is in front of you.

Trends drive most of what we do including eating. When it comes to making choices, all you want is something that is readily available, easy to prepare, looks good, and lastly taste good.

Mind Games

Food has powers to change your mood. What's the first thing that comes to mind when thinking of a birthday party? The cake? Right. What about your favorite memory of Thanksgiving? Is it the sweet potato pie? Or your aunt's famous macaroni and cheese? How about when your father stood over you and told you to eat your vegetables before you can get something to drink, or that time when a friend dared you to try spinach juice. Well, all these memories good or bad, triggers something to make you either love that certain food or hate it.
The mind has a way to play tricks on you. Sometimes, emotional feelings come out regarding food. Some people may find great comfort in eating their favorite foods, while some may be frightened by the thought of having that dessert after a meal.

Nutrition

The five groups are grain products (breads, cereals, rice, and pasta); vegetables; fruits; dairy, (yogurt, cheese); and the meat group, which includes meat, poultry, fish, dry beans, eggs, and nuts. The guidelines are as follows:

- Choose most of your **daily** foods from the grain products group (six to eleven servings); the vegetable group (three to five servings); and the fruit group (two to four servings);
- Eat moderate amounts of food from the milk group (two to three servings), and the meat group (two or three servings).

The Food Pyramid Guide provides recommendations that both vegetarians and non-vegetarians can use. Soy or almond milk would replace the dairy group for vegans. For vegetarians, legumes (beans, peas, and lentils), nuts and tofu can replace the solid foods in the meat group. Legumes work well in soups, casseroles and salads. With the information provided below you will learn all of the necessary terms to live a healthy lifestyle while providing the proper nutrients to your body.

Nutrient: A substance that provides nourishment essential for growth and the maintenance of life.

Nutrition: The process of providing or obtaining the food necessary for health and growth.

Malnutrition: Lack of proper nutrition.

The nutrients we put in our body changes during our lifecycle. For young adults we must make sure that we take nutrients that provide energy, and protein. Some nutrients that provide these are Vitamin C, K, B1, B2, and B3. The most important thing that you can do at this time is to cut out the processed foods and excessive sugar intake. These key terms will be a good reminder of the proper nutrients and the functions they serve.

Carbohydrates: A large group of organic compounds occurring in foods include sugars, starches, and fiber. Most carbohydrates come from plant-like foods. The main function of carbohydrates is to provide energy but also helps the body digest fats. The most common sources of carbohydrates are sugars, syrups, soft drinks, jams, jellies and candy.

Fats: A natural oily or greasy substance occurring in animal bodies are more commonly called lipids. All lipids contain fatty acids. Most fat in foods are visible. However, some are invisible like the fat in eggs and some cream products. Fats have many different functions. They area great source of energy, and also carry tons of flavors and make meat very tender.

Proteins: A large group of organic compounds that are composed called amino acids. Proteins are fundamental components of all living cells and include many substances such as enzymes, hormones, and antibodies that are necessary for the proper functioning of an organism. Your body needs amino acids from proteins for growth, maintenance, and repair of tissues. Children need more protein per pound because of their rapid growth. Most important sources of protein are poultry, fish, lean meats, milk, cheese, and eggs.

Vitamins: Are organic substances that are very important to the growth, reproduction, and metabolism of the body. They cannot be produced in the body but are found in certain foods. Eating a well balanced diet will insure the proper amount of vitamins needed.

> **Vitamin A** also known as retinol is essential for growth of teeth and bones. The main sources for

vitamin A are in foods such as milk, liver, and egg yolks. Darker color vegetables and fruits normally carry a higher value of vitamin A.

Vitamin D is also great for the growth of bones and teeth in adults. The main two sources of vitamin D would be in most fatty fish and all milk products. The most interesting thing about this vitamin is that the body can produce this with exposure to sunlight. Therefore, it's very important to use sunscreen when you are going in the sun for a long time. However, if you drink milk your body will produce enough Vitamin D.

Vitamin E mainly functions as a dietary antioxidant that reduces the harmful effects of oxygen on normal body functions. Vitamin E also keeps oxygen from reacting with red and white blood cells. Heart disease and cancer have been caused by too much oxygen exposure. Good sources of this vitamin are salad oils, fats, eggs, leafy green vegetables, and other variety meats.

Vitamin K helps the liver produce a substance that clots the blood in our bodies. Bacteria in the human intestinal tract can make vitamin K. Leafy green vegetables and cauliflowers are good sources of vitamin K.

Lastly and probably, the most important vitamin that I will mention is **Vitamin C**, which performs many functions in the body. It is important for healthy skin, teeth, bones, and blood vessels. It also helps the body fight infections and acts as a dietary antioxidant. Citrus fruits, strawberries, and melons are good sources as well as leafy vegetables, green peppers, broccoli and cabbage.

Thiamin known as vitamin B1, this vitamin is a part of B complex vitamins and is essential for the breakdown of carbohydrates. The main function of this vitamin is to help maintain a healthy appetite and digestion. The main sources for this vitamin are wheat germ, and pork products.

Riboflavin known as vitamin B2 is also a part of B complex vitamins and is responsible for the breakdown of carbohydrates, but the main function of this vitamin is to keep your skin smooth and prevent cracked lips. The main sources of this vitamin are all milk products, also oysters.

Lastly the importance of **H20** better known as **WATER**, a person can live without food for up to a month but only three to five days without water. The functions of water in your body are many. Most important of all, water moistens tissues in your mouth, nose and eyes. It also helps prevent constipation and regulates your body temperature. Your body takes the water from the foods and liquids you drink and eat. That's why it's important to drink more fluids that contain a lot of water if not straight water. Water is also important because it flushes your system out and rids your kidney and liver of all the bad stuff. Your body needs 64 ounces of water per day.

"Chef DAS"

**Chapter VIII
An Apple a Day Will
Keep the Doctor Away**

In this section you will learn the impact that certain foods have on the mind, body, and soul. Now I must say this first, I am no doctor and in no way shape or form recommend that you do not see a doctor if you are ever feeling ill. The foods that I list below are some preventative suggestions that can be taken into consideration.

Apples: may help protect your heart, prevent constipation, block diarrhea, improve lung capacity, and cushion joints.

Apricots: may help combat cancer, control blood pressure, save your eyesight, shield against Alzheimer's, and slow aging process.

Artichokes: may help aid digestion, lower cholesterol, protect your heart, stabilize blood sugar and guard against liver disease.

Avocados: may help battle diabetes, lower cholesterol, stop strokes, control blood pressure, and make skin smooth.

Bananas: may protect your heart, quiet a cough, strengthen bones, control blood pressure and block diarrhea.

Beans: may prevent constipation, help hemorrhoids, lower cholesterol, combat cancer, and stabilize blood sugar.

Beets: may help control blood pressure, combat cancer, strengthen bones, protect your heart, and aid weight loss.

Blueberries: may help fight the bacteria that causes diarrhea, combat cancer, protect your heart, stabilize blood sugar, and boost memory.

Broccoli: may help strengthen bones, protect eyesight, combat cancer, protect your heart, and control blood pressure.

Cabbage: may help combat cancer, prevent constipation, promote weight loss, protect your heart, and help hemorrhoids.

Cantaloupe: may help eyesight, control blood pressure, lower cholesterol, combat cancer, and support immune system.

Carrots: may help your eyes, protect your heart, prevent constipation, combat cancer, and promote weight loss.

Caffeine: may have a positive effect on cognitive functioning, including your ability to pay attention, your psychomotor skills, and your memory.

Cauliflower: may help protect against prostate cancer, combat breast cancer, strengthen bones, banish bruises, and guard against heart disease.

Cherries: may help protect your heart, combat cancer, end insomnia, slow aging process, and shield against Alzheimer's.

Chestnuts: may help promote weight loss, protect your heart, lower cholesterol, combat cancer, and improve your blood pressure.

Chili peppers: may help digestion, soothe sore throat, clear sinuses, combat cancer and boost your immune system.

Figs: may help promote weight loss, stop strokes and lower cholesterol.

Fish: is good for your brain and may help boost your memory and support the immune system. A minimal deficiency of zinc impairs thinking and memory.

Flax: may help digestion, battle diabetes, improve mental health and boost your immune system.

Garlic: may help kill flu and cold viruses, fight fungus, control blood pressure and combat cancer.

Ginger root: may help fight nausea.

Grapefruit: may help protect against heart attacks, promotes weight loss, helps stops strokes, combats prostate cancer, and lowers cholesterol.

Grapes: may help with eyesight, conquer kidney stones, combat cancer, enhance blood flow, and protect your heart.

Green Tea: may help fight cancer, protect your heart, stop strokes, promote weight loss and kill bacteria.

Honey: may help heal wounds, aid digestion, guard against ulcers, increase energy and fight allergies.

Lemons/Limes: may help combat cancer; protect your heart, control blood pressure, and smooth skin.

Mangoes: may help combat cancer, boost memory, regulate thyroid, aid digestion and shield against Alzheimer's.

Mushrooms: may help control blood pressure, lower cholesterol, kill bacteria, combat cancer and strengthen bones.

Oats: may help lower cholesterol, combat cancer, battle diabetes, prevent constipation and make skin smooth.

Olive Oil: may help protect your heart, promote weight loss, fight cancer and battle diabetes.

Onions: may help reduce risk of heart attack, kill bacteria, lower cholesterol, and fight fungus.

Oranges: may help boost the immune system, fight cancer, protect your heart, and strengthens respiration.

Peaches: may help prevent constipation, stop strokes, aid digestion and hemorrhoids.

Peanuts: may help protect against heart disease, promote weight loss, fight prostate cancer, and lower cholesterol.

Pineapples: may help strengthen bones, relieve colds, aid digestion, dissolve warts and block diarrhea.

Prunes: may helps low aging process, prevent constipation, boost memory, lower cholesterol and protect against heart disease.

Rice: may help protect your heart, battle diabetes, conquer kidney stones, fight cancer, and stop strokes.

Strawberries: may help fight cancer, protect your heart, boost memory and calm stress.

Sweet potatoes: may help your eyesight, lift your mood, fight cancer and strengthen bones.

Tomatoes: may help protect your prostate, combat cancer, lower cholesterol and protect your heart.

Walnuts: may help lower cholesterol, fight cancer, boost memory, lift moods and protect against heart disease.

Watermelon: may help protect prostate, promote weight loss, lower cholesterol, stop strokes and control blood pressure.

Wheat: may help fight colon cancer, prevents constipation, lower cholesterol, help stop strokes and improve digestion.

Yogurt: may help fight the bacteria that cause vaginal yeast infections and guards against ulcers.

"Chef DAS"

**Chapter IX
Eating Out**

When eating out, you want to remember that the bigger and better the menu, the more likely your chances of finding healthy suggestions. You will notice that most fast food places have a small menu of healthy choices. If so, order a side salad instead of the French fries.

In any type of restaurant, read the menu descriptions that give you valuable advice on the various options. Most foods are very high in sodium, sugars, and fat. All foods tossed in butter such as pasta or vegetables and even fish that are broiled in butter are not the best choices for your diet. Foods that are served with cheese sauce or gravy, or fried or breaded are most likely high in fat content. Foods that are served with barbeque sauce, smoked food and even soup are all very likely high in sodium.

The best way to feel secure in the food you eat while out is to order your food a particular way so that the person who is making your food takes special care. For health conscious menu selections, choose foods prepared with low-fat cooking methods or order your food without salt or butter. You can always order dressings and sauces on the side to add just enough flavor rather than smoother your food. Fresh vegetable salads are always a great option. Just be careful of the toppings you add. For dessert, choose low- fat options or fresh fruit. The food you eat affects your caloric intake as well as your fat, sugar, and sodium consumption.

A good way to monitor the food you eat out without looking weird while ordering is to consider ordering an appetizer instead of entrée. This will keep you from eating more than you intended. Consider having water with your meal instead of a soft drink. This choice will save you money as well as calories from added sugars.

Did you know? The average American spends roughly $200 per month eating 16-18 meals prepared outside the home. That means that the average American spends around $11 dollars per meal. I am sure your lunch usually costs less than dinner but however you look at it that is a lot of money. If you go to the grocery store to buy food you can purchase a full meal for under $5. Things that make you go hmmmm.

Here are some helpful tips to save money:

Eat Healthy: Fruit and vegetables are cheaper than eating other convenient snacks like chips, candies, and cookies. Grabbing an apple or banana for a quick snack is cheaper and healthier. Apples have nutrients you need, fewer calories and actually keep you full. A bag of Cheetos will cost you more than a piece of fruit and is loaded with tons of fat and empty calories.

Plan your meals: If you plan your meals and keep track of what food items you have in your pantry, freezer or fridge, you are less likely to make another trip to the store.

Find Sales: If you know what stores have the best sales and deals in your area, you are guaranteed to save some money while shopping.

Never EVER go to the grocery store on an Empty Stomach: If you have not eaten a meal in a long time and go to the grocery store, you certainly are going to spend a lot more money than expected. When your stomach is grumbling, everything in the store looks good and you will buy more food than you need and spend too much money. Make sure you make a grocery list before you go to the store so that you do not buy more than you need. Remember what you actually need.

"Chef DAS"

Chapter X
How Long Does It Live?

In this chapter you will learn about the storage of food and the estimated time it has to live in your home. This information will be helpful for all young adults who have always wondered the estimated shelf life of food.

Herbs and Spices (Dried)

Allspice: 2-3 years
Basil: 1-3 years
Bay leaves: 1-3 years
Black pepper: 2-3 years
Chili powder: 2-3 years
Cinnamon sticks: 3-4 years
Cinnamon (ground): 2-3years
Cloves (ground): 2-3 years
Coriander seed: 3-4 years
Coriander (ground): 2-3 years
Cumin: 2-3 years
Dill: 1-3 years
Dry mustard: 2-3 years
Garlic (minced): 2 years unopened
Garlic (whole): 3-4 months
Garlic powder: 2-3 years
Ginger (ground): 2-3 years
Marjoram: 1-3 years
Nutmeg: 2-3 years
Onion powder: 2-3 years
Oregano: 1-3 years
Parsley: 1-3 years
Pepper (black or white): 3-4 years
Rosemary: 1-3 years
Sage: 1-3 years
Seasoned Salt: 1 year
Savory: 1-3 years

Thyme: 1-3 years

Canned Goods

Applesauce: 12-18 months
Canned beans: 2-5 years
Broth (beef, chicken, vegetable): 2-5 years
Canned fruit: 12-18 months
Canned meats (tuna, salmon, chicken): 2-5 years
Pumpkin puree: 12-18 months
Soup (except tomato): 1-2 years
Soup (tomato): 12 months
Tomato paste: 12 months
Tomatoes (crushed): 12 months
Tomatoes (stewed): 12 months
Tomatoes (sundried): 12 months

Baking Supplies

Baking Powder: 18 months
Baking Soda: 2 years
Chocolate Chips (Semi-sweet): 2 years
Cocoa: 1 year
Coconut: 12 months unopened; 6 months opened; refrigerate after opening
Corn Meal: 6-12 months
Corn Starch: 18 months
Flour (all purpose): 6-8 months
Flour (wheat): 6-8 months
Honey: Indefinitely
Milk (evaporated): 1 year
Milk (powdered): 1 year

Milk (sweetened condensed): 1 year
Molasses: 2 years
Nuts (shelled): 4 months
Nuts (unshelled): 6 months
Oil (canola): 2 years unopened, 1 year opened
Oil (olive): 6 months
Oil (vegetable spray): 2 years
Salt: Indefinitely
Sugar (brown): Indefinitely
Sugar (granulated): Indefinitely
Sugar (powdered): Indefinitely
Vanilla extract (imitation): 3 years
Vanilla extract (real): Indefinitely
Yeast: Follow expiration date on package

Dried Goods

Cookies: 2 months
Crackers: 8 months
Dried beans: 1 year
Dried fruit: 6-12 months
Gelatin: 18 months
Grits: 1year
Lentils: 1 year
Oatmeal: 1 year
Popcorn Kernels: 2 years
Pretzels/Chips: 2 months
Toaster pastries: 6 months
Tortillas: 3 months

Pasta and Grains

Egg noodles: 6 months
Pasta: 2 years
Rice (basmati): 2 years

Rice (brown): 6 months
Rice (jasmine): 2 years
Rice (white): 2 years
Rice (wild): 6 months

Condiments

Barbeque sauce: 1 year
Hot sauce: 4 years unopened
Jelly: 2 years
Ketchup: 1 year
Maple syrup: 1 year
Mayonnaise: 3-4 months after package date
Mustard: 2 years
Peanut butter: 6-9 months unopened, 3 months opened
Pickles: 1 year
Salad dressing: 12 months
Salsa: 12 months
Soy sauce: 3 years unopened
Vinegar (apple cider, malt, red wine, rice, white wine, white): 2 years
Vinegar (balsamic): 3 years
Worcestershire sauce: 1 year

Frozen Food

Bacon: 1-2 months
Chicken or turkey (whole): 1 year
Chicken pieces: 9 months

Chops (pork): 4 -12 months
Fish: 3-8 months
Ground meats: 3-4 months
Ham: 1-2 months
Hot dogs: 1-2 months
Lunch meat: 3-4 months
Roast: 4-12 months
Sausage: 1-2 months
Shellfish: 3-12 months
Steak: 6-12 months
Butter: 6-9 months
Cheese (blocked): 6 months
Cheese (shredded): 2-3 months
Egg whites: 12 months
Eggs (shelled): 12 months
Ice cream: 2-4 months
Milk: 3 months

Refrigerated Food

Bacon: 7 days
Butter: 1-3 months
Cheese: 1-2 months
Chicken or Turkey: 1-2 days
Chops (pork): 3-5 days
Eggs: 3-5 weeks
Fish and Shellfish: 1-2 days uncooked, 3-5 days cooked
Ground beef or turkey: 1-2 days
Ham (cooked) sliced: 3-4 days
Hot dogs: 2 weeks unopened, 1 week opened
Lunch meat: 2 weeks unopened, 3-5 days opened
Milk: Follow the expiration date on carton
Sausage: 1-2 days uncooked
Sour cream: 1-3 weeks
Steak: 3-5 days

Yogurt: 1-2 weeks

Beverages

Coffee (ground): 1 year unopened, 1-2 weeks opened
Coffee (instant): 1 year unopened, 2-3 months opened
Iced tea mix: 3 years unopened, 6-12 months opened
Juice boxes: 4 months
Juice (bottled or canned): 12 months
Soda: 3 months after expiration date
Tea in bags: 18 months unopened, 1 year opened
Water (bottled): 1-2 years

Chapter XI
Breakfast

Panny-Cakes

Mise en place (Everything in place):

2 cups all-purpose flour
2 1/2 teaspoons baking powder
3 tablespoons granulated sugar
1/2 teaspoon salt
1 tablespoon vanilla extract
2 large eggs
1 1/2 to 1 3/4 cups milk
2 tablespoons melted butter

Preparation:
1. The first thing you want to do is mix flour, baking powder, sugar, and salt together in a mixing bowl and set aside.
2. In a separate bowl, whisk together the eggs, vanilla extract, and 1 1/2 cups of milk.
3. Add the milk and eggs mixture to the flour mixture, stirring until smooth without any lumps in batter.
4. Blend in melted butter. If the batter seems too thick to pour, add a little more milk.
5. Cook on a hot, greased non-stick pan or griddle. For medium size pancakes use 3-4 Tablespoons (1/4 cup) of batter for each pancake. Cook until bubbles begin to form around the edges.
6. Cook until a golden brown color forms and flip on the other side and do the same. Once finished, glaze with melted butter.

Best served with warm maple syrup.

Serves 4.

Good Ol' Fashion Shrimp and Grits

Mise en place:

For the Shrimp:
¼ cup butter or oil
¼ cup, plus 1 tablespoon flour
1 pound shrimp, peeled and deveined
1 onion, finely chopped
1 bell pepper, finely chopped
3 garlic cloves, minced
1 ½ cups chicken broth
2 chopped scallions
Salt and pepper to taste

For the Grits:
3 cups chicken broth or water
1 cup heavy cream
1 cup quick grits
1 ½ cups shredded cheddar cheese
1 teaspoon salt

Preparation:

1. Heat the butter or oil in a skillet over medium-low flame. Whisk in the ¼ cup flour and cook slowly, stirring frequently, until the flour turns a deep reddish brown, cook anywhere from 15 to 20 minutes. Be sure not to burn. This is your roux.
2. While the roux is cooking, mix the shrimp together in a bowl with the 1 tablespoon of flour remaining, salt and pepper. Set aside.

3. Stir the onion and peppers into the roux and cook for 2 or 3 minutes, or until the onions soften and become translucent. Stir in the garlic and cook for another 30 seconds. Finally, stir in the shrimp and cook for another minute or so.
4. Whisk in the chicken stock and reduce heat to low. Simmer for 2 to 3 minutes, or until the sauce thickens. Adjust seasoning and set aside while you make your grits.
5. Bring the chicken broth or water, cream and salt to a boil in a saucepan over medium flame. Slowly stir in the grits. Cover; reduce heat to low, and cook, stirring occasionally, for 5 to 6 minutes. For creamier grits, add a little more cream.
6. Put a scoop of grits into each serving bowl and top with the shrimp and its sauce. Garnish with chopped scallions and serve hot.

Serves 4.

Strawberry French Toast

Mise en place:

For the French toast:
4 eggs
1 teaspoon sugar
1 teaspoon ground cinnamon
1 teaspoon salt
1 cup milk
1 tablespoon vanilla extract
8 slices white bread
1 stick butter

For the strawberry sauce:
2 cups fresh strawberries
1 cup sugar
1 tablespoon cornstarch
¼ cup water

Preparation:

1. Break eggs into shallow bowl; beat lightly with a fork. Stir in sugar, cinnamon, vanilla, salt, and milk.
2. Over medium-low heat, heat griddle or non stick pan coated with a thin layer of butter or margarine.
3. Place the bread slices, one at a time, into the bowl, Begin to let the slices soak up egg mixture for a few seconds, then carefully turn to coat the other side. Soak only as many slices as you will be cooking at one time. If you over-soak the bread you will run the risk of your bread turning soggy and falling apart.

"Chef DAS"

4. Place bread slices on your hot griddle or pan searing until bottom is golden brown. Turn and brown the other side. Repeat this step until all bread slices are cooked. Serve French toast hot with butter and strawberry sauce.
5. Wash the strawberries and remove the stems cut in halves.
6. In a small pot place strawberries, sugar, water and bring to a boil stirring frequently. Add the cornstarch in the water until it dissolves and pour into the sauce while stirring. This will begin to thicken. Let the sauce cool and serve.

Serves 4.

Chicken and Waffles

Mise en place:

For the waffles:
2 cups all purpose flour
1 ½ teaspoon salt
3 ½ teaspoons baking powder
2 tablespoons white sugar
2 eggs
1 ¾ cups milk
1/3 cup melted butter
1 ½ teaspoon vanilla extract
1can non-stick vegetable spray

For the chicken:
1 (2pound) Chicken cut into pieces
2 cups all purpose flour
3 tablespoons yellow mustard
¼ cup chopped fresh parsley
2 tablespoons Lawry's seasoned salt
1 tablespoon ground black pepper
Oil for frying (canola)

Preparation:

1. Preheat waffle oven to medium heat or desired temperature.
2. In a medium size-mixing bowl, mix together flour, salt, baking powder and sugar. (Set aside)
3. In a separate bowl, beat the eggs. Stir in the milk, butter and vanilla. Combine the milk mixture and the flour mixture. Stir until smooth and lump free.
4. Pour the batter evenly into the preheated waffle iron. Cook the waffles until golden

brown and fluffy. Serve hot with melted butter and maple syrup.
5. In large mixing bowl combine chicken pieces, seasoned salt, pepper, parsley, and yellow mustard. Mix well until mustard coats the chicken.
6. Add flour to bowl, mix well until all chicken pieces are entirely coated with flour.
7. Heat oil in a deep pot at 350°degrees F. Fill pot only ½ way to ¾ full of oil.
8. Once oil is hot (sprinkle pinch of flour in oil. If it bubbles, it is hot), slowly drop chicken pieces in oil without crowding the pot. Make sure that the oil covers the chicken.
9. Fry the chicken until it reaches a golden brown color. Dark meat typically takes a little longer to cook 12-14 minutes, White meat 8-10.
10. Place fried chicken on paper towel lined plate to drain excess oil. Serve hot.

Serves 5.

Note: prepare waffle batter and set in fridge. Once chicken is half way done, start cooking waffles.

Vegetable Quiche

Mise en place:

1 (9-inch) baked pie shell
3 tablespoons butter
1 onion, chopped
1 green pepper, chopped
1½ cup cherry tomatoes cut in halves
½ cup mushrooms, sliced
5 eggs
¼ cup milk
1/3 cup shredded cheddar
Salt and pepper to taste

Preparation:

1. Preheat oven to 350°degrees.
2. Smooth butter on the outer edge of the piecrust.
3. In a non-stick pan melt butter over medium heat; cook onions, green peppers, tomatoes, and mushrooms until soft. Set aside to cool
4. In a medium size mixing bowl beat eggs and slowly add milk. Stir in parmesan cheese.
5. Pour vegetables into pie shell and slowly add egg mixture.
6. Bake in preheated oven until a knife inserted in the center comes out clean. 35-40 minutes. Let cool before serving.

Serves 6.

*Note: In this recipe, the vegetables are interchangeable.

Notes

Chapter XII
Lunch

"Chef DAS"

Tuna and Pepper Melt

Mise en place:

2 cans (each 6 ounces/170g) tuna, drained
half sweet red pepper, diced
1 stalk celery
2 green onions
2 tablespoons light mayonnaise
2 tablespoons plain yogurt or sour cream
1 tablespoon drained capers
½ teaspoon ground cumin
½ teaspoon pepper
¼ teaspoon salt
¼ teaspoon cayenne pepper
4 soft Panini (Italian) buns
½ cup shredded cheddar or Swiss cheese

Preparation:

1. In a bowl, mix together tuna, red pepper, celery, green onions, mayonnaise, plain yogurt, capers, cumin, pepper, salt and cayenne pepper.
2. Cut buns in half horizontally; spread tuna mixture evenly over bottom half of each. Sprinkle each evenly with cheese. Replace bun top.
3. In nonstick skillet or grill, cook sandwiches over medium heat, pressing often to flatten and turning once, for about 5 minutes or until crisp and cheese is melted.

Serves 4.

We in the Club Turkey Sandwich

Mise en place:

1 cup mayonnaise
1/4 cup honey mustard
3 tablespoons balsamic vinaigrette
½ sliced yellow onion
¼ cup olive oil
4 crisp leaves of romaine or iceberg lettuce
12 slices smoked turkey breast
8 slices Swiss cheese
16 slices thick cut bacon, cooked and drained
1 tomato, cut into 2 slices per sandwich
8 slices sourdough
3 tablespoons butter, softened

Preparation:

1. Sauté sliced onions in non-stick pan until clear. Set aside and let cool.
2. Spread mayonnaise and mustard on bread slices.
3. Place 3 turkey slices, onions, 2 cheese slices, 4 bacon slices, lettuce and 2 tomato slices on half of the bread slices.
4. Drizzle balsamic dressing on ingredients
5. Add remaining bread slice, place mayo sides down, on tops of sandwiches.

Spread the outsides of sandwiches with butter.

Brown in a skillet or grill on medium heat until bread is golden in color.

Serves 4.

Chicken Kabobs

Mise en place:

2 each - 8 oz boneless skinless chicken breast
1 green bell pepper
1 red bell pepper
1 yellow onion
1 pack cherry tomatoes
1 pack 6 inch wooden skewers
1 teaspoon Salt
1 teaspoon black pepper
2 tablespoons oil

Preparation:

1. Dice chicken and vegetables (peppers and onions) into medium-sized cuts.
2. Assemble chicken and vegetables onto skewers in chicken-veggie-chicken-veggie format. Finish each skewer with 1 cherry tomato.
3. Season kabob with salt and pepper, drizzle with oil.

4. Sear kabobs on flattop grill over medium heat, 3 minutes each side or until golden brown color.
5. Finish kabobs in preheated 350-degree oven until chicken juice runs clear (no longer than 12 minutes).

Serves 4-6.

Shrimp Lettuce Cups

Mise en place:

16 Boston Bibb or iceberg lettuce
1 pound medium size peeled and deveined shrimp
1 tablespoon vegetable oil
1 large onion, chopped
2 cloves fresh garlic, minced
1 tablespoon soy sauce
¼ cup hoisin sauce
2 teaspoons pickled ginger, minced
1 tablespoon rice wine vinegar
1 bunch green onions, chopped
2 teaspoons sesame oil

Preparation:

1. Rinse whole lettuce leaves and pat dry, being careful not to tear them. Set aside.
2. In a medium skillet over high heat, Sauté shrimp in 1 tablespoon cooking oil, stirring often and reducing the heat to medium, Cook the onion in the same pan, stirring frequently.

Add the garlic, soy sauce, hoisin sauce, ginger, and vinegar to the onions and shrimp, stir.
3. Stir green onions, and sesame oil. Continue cooking until the onions just begin to wilt, about 2 minutes.
4. Arrange lettuce leaves around the outer edge of a large serving platter, and pile meat mixture in the center. To serve, allow each person to spoon a portion of the meat into a lettuce leaf. Wrap the lettuce around the meat like a burrito, and enjoy! Serves 4.

Vegetable Panini

Mise en place:

¼ cup mayonnaise
2 teaspoons fresh chives, chopped
1 teaspoon sugar
1 carrot, peeled and sliced lengthwise into 1/8" strips
1 small zucchini, sliced into 1/8" strips
1 yellow summer squash, sliced into 1/8" strips
1 red bell pepper, sliced thin
1 small red onion, peeled and thinly sliced
¼ cup olive oil
¼ cup tarragon vinegar
2 slices of pepper jack cheese
Salt and pepper to taste
4 slices of Panini bread (or bread of choice)

Preparation:

1. In small bowl, combine mayonnaise, and 2 teaspoon fresh chives. Mix well, cover and refrigerate.
2. Place sliced vegetables in a zip-lock plastic bag and season with salt and pepper. In small bowl mix 1/4 cup olive oil and 1/4 cup tarragon vinegar. Drizzle half of this mixture over the vegetables in the plastic bag. Set aside for a few minutes to marinate.
3. Prepare and preheat two sided grill. Place vegetables on grill and cook 3 minutes, until tender. Reduce grill heat to medium-low. Brush panini bread slices with remaining olive oil and tarragon vinegar mixture and grill 2 minutes per side, until golden brown.
4. Spread each slice of bread with the chive mayonnaise, and then form sandwiches with the grilled vegetables. Add sliced cheese and grill again for 1-2 minutes until compressed and hot.

Serves 2.

"Chef DAS"

Crab Cakes

Mise en place:

4 tablespoons mayonnaise
1 tablespoon fresh parsley, finely chopped
1 tablespoon green onion, finely chopped
2 teaspoons red bell pepper, minced
1 lemon
1 egg
1 pound (can) lump or claw crab meat
1 ¼ cup fresh bread crumbs
3 tablespoons vegetable oil
Salt and pepper to taste

Preparation:

1. Combine mayonnaise, parsley, and seasonings; set aside.
2. Drain crabmeat; gently squeeze to get as much of the liquid out as possible. Put crabmeat in a bowl. With a spatula or wooden spoon, fold in mayonnaise mixture, egg and 1 cup of the bread crumbs, just until blended. Mix well.
3. Shape into 8 crab cakes, about 2 1/2 inches in diameter. (I use a cookie cutter or a ring mold with an open top to shape the cakes and press the ingredients down to make them hold together.) Coat gently into ¼ bread crumbs. Cover and chill for 1 hour.
4. Heat oil over medium heat. Fry crab cakes for about 5 minutes on each side or until golden

brown, carefully turning only once. Serve with lemon wedges.

Serves 4.

"Chef DAS"

Notes

Chapter XIII
Dinner

Chicken Roulade stuffed with spinach, carrots, and mozzarella cheese served over pan fried potatoes

Mise en place:

2 chicken breasts, butter fried (sliced down the center horizontally without cutting through)
1 tablespoon olive oil, plus ½ cup olive oil, divided
2 cups fresh washed spinach
1 log of fresh mozzarella cheese, sliced into 2 inch long strips
1 peeled carrot, thinly cut into julienne strips
2 Idaho potatoes, sliced 1/8 inch thick
1 cup chicken broth
Salt and pepper to taste

Preparation:

1. Preheat the oven to 350° degrees F.
2. With a meat mallet, pound butter fried chicken breast until thin. Put chicken on a large piece of plastic wrap and season chicken with salt and pepper, to taste.
3. In a sauté pan over medium heat, heat 1 tablespoon oil and sauté the vegetables until tender. Arrange the vegetables and mozzarella cheese in center of chicken breast. Roll each chicken into a log and wrap tightly in the plastic wrap. Tie the ends of the wrap into a knot. Cover the bottom of a shallow baking dish with water and add the chicken. Bake until cooked through, about 20 minutes.
4. Meanwhile, heat a large sauté pan over medium-high heat; add the remaining 1/2 cup

of olive oil. When the oil is hot, add the potatoes and fry until golden brown. Remove from the oil to paper towels to drain. Season with salt and pepper, to taste.
5. In small saucepot over medium heat, reduce chicken broth until broth thickens.
6. Remove the chicken from the oven to a cutting board. Discard the plastic wrap and slice. Arrange the potatoes on serving plates and top with the chicken. Drizzle broth over chicken.

Serves 2.

"Chef DAS"

Pan Seared Salmon

Mise en place:

2 7 oz salmon filets
1 oz olive oil
1 teaspoon basil, chiffonade
½ teaspoon chopped garlic
1 teaspoon minced onion
1 can artichokes cut in chunks
1 cup fresh washed spinach
1 oz chicken or vegetable stock
1 tablespoon whole butter
Salt and pepper to taste

Preparation:

1. Pre-heat a non stick pan, pour in olive oil.
2. Season salmon with salt, pepper, and basil. Place salmon flesh side down and sear in hot pan. Remove salmon from pan, and finish in the oven for about 7 minutes.
3. In same pan, sauté minced garlic and onions; add artichokes, and glaze with chicken stock. Toss in Spinach and whole butter; adjust with salt and pepper.

Serves 2.

Lean Mean Turkey Meatloaf

Mise en place:

1-2 packages extra lean ground turkey (or ground beef)
2 eggs
Packaged breadcrumbs
Barbecue sauce
½ cup green bell pepper
½ cup onion
½ cup mushroom

Preparation:

1. Pre heat oven 350° degrees F.
2. Combine meat, eggs, and other ingredients mix well with hands, slowly add breadcrumbs to thicken the loaf.
3. Form into a bread loaf shape. Bake until thoroughly cooked about 25 to 30 minutes at 350° degrees.
4. Glaze with barbecue sauce, place back in oven for 2 minutes.
5. Let cool and remove from pan, slice thin.

Serves 4-6.

"Chef DAS"

Potato Crusted Halibut

Mise en place:

2 7 oz halibut
½ cup seasoned potato flakes
¼ cup red peppers
¼ cup roasted yellow peppers
1 cup fresh washed spinach
1 shallot, minced
1 garlic clove, minced
5 button mushrooms, sliced
¼ stick of butter
½ cup chicken or vegetable stock
3 tablespoons vegetable oil
Salt and Pepper to taste

Preparation:

1. Preheat Oven at 350° degrees F.
2. Season fish with salt and pepper. Preheat nonstick pan and pour in oil.
3. Coat halibut in potato flakes until the fish is completely covered.
4. Sear fish on both sides until potato flakes turn a golden brown color.
5. Place Fish in preheated oven continue cooking for 12 minutes.
6. In same pan, sauté peppers, mushrooms, spinach, shallots and garlic on medium heat for 7 minutes or until the peppers are soft.

7. Once your vegetables are cooked, glaze your pan with chicken or vegetable stock and smooth with butter.
8. Plate sauce and vegetables in a large plate or bowl and place cooked fish on top.

Serves 2.

Chicken Stir-Fry

Mise en place:

2 7oz boneless skinless chicken breast
½ cup broccoli
1 red bell red pepper
1 green bell pepper
½ cup yellow onion
2 tablespoons sprouts
½ teaspoon seasoned salt
¾ cup soy sauce
2 tablespoon olive oil
Salt and pepper to taste

Preparation:

1. Cut chicken into strips and season. Set aside.
2. Cut vegetables into julienne strips.
3. In a nonstick pan, add 2 tablespoons of oil. Brown chicken until done or juices run clear.
4. Add vegetables to pan, and more oil if necessary. Sauté to desired tenderness.
5. Add Soy sauce. Pour over Rice.

Serves 2-3.

"Chef DAS"

Steak Fajita Wrap

Mise en place

8 ounce flank steak
1 ounce vegetable oil
2 12 inch flour tortillas, warmed
¼ cup sour cream
1 avocado, diced
1 cup cooked rice
3 tablespoons salsa
2 tablespoons onion, diced
1 tablespoon fresh cilantro, chopped
¼ cup shredded cheddar cheese
Salt and pepper to taste

Preparation:

1. Place the vegetable oil in a heavy frying pan over medium heat.
2. Season the flank steak with salt and pepper.
3. Place the flank steak in the frying pan and cook on high heat for three minutes on each side.
4. Remove the flank steak, let rest and slice thinly.

To assemble the wrap:
Lay the two warmed flour tortillas out flat and place the following ingredients into the center of each tortilla.

4 ounces of flank steak

2 tablespoons sour cream
½ avocado, diced
½ cup rice
1 tablespoon salsa
2 tablespoons shredded cheddar cheese
1 tablespoon diced onions
½ tablespoon fresh cilantro, chopped

Method: Fold in one side of tortilla and then roll closed, folding in the top and bottom edges so that all ingredients are enclosed in tortilla.

Serves 2.

Notes

Afterword

This brings us to the end. I hope that after reading this, you will hit the kitchen confidently. The main goal for writing this book was to create a helpful guide that would provide useful knowledge and ignite culinary inspiration. I know that you will be a culinary superstar in no time. "Now Look Who's Cooking." You are.

Please visit www.chefdas.com for more information.

Thank you for reading; Chef Das debut release; *"Now Look Who's Cooking"* and be sure to leave a review. More titles available @ www.Printhousebooks.com

PRINTHOUSE BOOKS
Read it, Enjoy it, Tell a friend.
VIP INK Publishing Group, Incorporated.
Atlanta, GA
www.PrintHouseBooks.com

www.ingramcontent.com/pod-product-compliance
Lightning Source LLC
Chambersburg PA
CBHW070053120426
42742CB00048B/2505